A Simpler Thyme in the Kitchen

Generally when one thinks of comfort, satisfaction, giving and fulfillment, their mind and belly head to the kitchen. What better place to show that love and gratitude for your family and the bounty of the garden than in your very own kitchen?

This appreciation comes in many different forms: pies, cakes, salads, soups and the list could go on for days. But, the underlying love from the hands that tended the garden, harvested and preserved the food, and knowingly prepared each dish, that love is the secret ingredient that gives the most flavor. This cookbook is just that. It is a collection of farm to table recipes collected over generational decades from the amazing women in my family. My sweet mother, Mickey, my grandmothers, Edna and Villa, plus other dear family members, and yours truly. Each recipe contains our own unique thumbprint of creativity, inspiration, ancestral wisdom, but above all else, love. May you develop and add your own touch of love to these family entrusted recipes, to bring gratitude, thanksgiving and memories to your own family.

To this very day, some fifty plus years later, I can still smell the content that was once contained in my Grandma Edna's spice cupboard. I can picture her small frame standing at her kitchen sink, tirelessly canning her special Christmas beets. Or my mother carefully stirring and keeping watch over a bubbling kettle of her spaghetti sauce, transforming our small kitchen into a fine Italian restaurant. More often than not, it is food that transports us back in time to a simpler day... A Simpler Thyme in the Kitchen. Herbal Blessings!

Table of Contents:

5	Herbs and Their Beneficial Properties
8	Infusions vs. Decoctions
9	Spring
13	Herbal Fun Facts
17	Eggucation
24	Potato - Potatoe
25	Summer
33	History of the Mango - Green pepper confusion
37	Garden Folk Lore
48	Food for Thought...
49	Autumn
51	Lets Get to the "Core" with a Little Apple History
53	Harvest Blessings
56	Jack-o-Lanterns
67	Winter
69	Christmas the Most "Wonderful" Time of the Year
79	Root Vegetables
83	Forget-Us-Not
85	Dressings
89	Cooking Conversions
90	Index

Get to know the three local women that collaborated to make this lovely collection of recipes, folklore and history, photographs and artwork a reality.

About the author: Julia Brown - Certified Master Herbalist - Fresno, Ohio

My interest in the kitchen and the garden, inspired by the women in my life, quickly accelerated my desire and passion for all things herb related. Which in turn fueled my journey to become a Certified Master Herbalist. Fortunately for me, my loving husband of 35 years and our 2 children all support my love and use of herbs both in the kitchen and medicinally speaking. We are blessed to operate a small herbal education cabin here in rural Coshocton County Ohio, A Simpler Thyme Ltd. which expresses that connection of farm-to-table and table-to-soul lifestyle.

This cookbook and collection of recipes has long been a brain child of mine, that I'm thrilled to see come to life. I am a firm believer that our Heavenly Father put all things on this good earth for our benefit, herbs being one of them. After all, like my Mother often said "you are what you eat" and to quote Hippocrates "food should be thy medicine and medicine should be thy food", both being of sound advice. It is my sincere pleasure and honor to bring my passion for food and herbs to others to experience and enjoy. As well as to spark an interest into the wonderful world of herbs and how they are linked to the food we eat and serve our families. I could dive into the depths of herbs: how to plant, nurture, wild craft, preserve and use their many benefits and properties, but that will have to wait for... A Simpler Thyme in the Garden! Herbal Blessings!

Find me at https://www.asimplerthyme.com or follow along on Facebook for herb class updates and herbalism tid-bits https://www.facebook.com/Asimplerthymeltd .

About the Designer & Photographer: Olivia Stock - Videographer & Studying Herbalist - Frazeysburg, Ohio

Olivia Stock is a nature lover, videographer and photographer. Her love of the outdoors blossomed as a child and has thrived in her adult years as she and her husband have explored 20 states together. Olivia is a studying herbalist who met Julia Brown while working at an apothecary, where they instantly became friends. When Julia mentioned the cookbook she'd been wanting to create for years, Olivia was immediately interested and wanted to help it come to life. After about a year of planning, cooking, and designing it's finally here and ready to share with the world!

To book a shoot or see her previous work, go to https://oliviastockdavis.my.canva.site/ or contact her on Instagram at @out.living .

About the Artist: Amy Casey - Watercolor Artist - Coshocton, Ohio

Amy Casey is an artist with a deep appreciation for fellow artists, teachers, and professors who have guided her art journey. She wants to give special recognition to her art mentor and dear friend, Thomas Nelson, for his wisdom and encouragement. Amy is grateful for the love and support of her husband Marc, her children, extended family and friends. She extends a big THANK YOU to Julia Brown for her friendship and generous offer to illustrate her cookbook.

Amy lives in Coshocton and creates artwork in her home studio. To view Amy's work or to request a commission or purchase artwork, visit her website at https://www.caseyarts.com/ .

Herbs and Their Beneficial Properties:

There is an amazing long and winding path into the world of herbs and all of their beneficial properties and many uses. However, within these pages I'm going to entice you to explore with me just a small window of their importance, gifts and wonders. Without saying, all herbs contain a bounty of antioxidants and a wonderful host of vitamins, minerals and nutrients; herbs truly can be a blessing to the kitchen and ones' household.

Basil – known as the "kingly or noble" herb, there are many types and varieties across the globe (too numerous to mention here) of this lovely herb. Basil was so valued, that in ancient times only Kings or Noblemen could possess her seeds. It was so highly valued in fact, that basil was once used as currency. When one thinks of basil, the three "P's" often come to mind: Pizza, Pasta & Pesto. However, she is so much more! Basil can be incorporated into a lovely herbal infusion to help ease headaches associated with stress and anxiety. She is calming and soothing and can help to decrease symptoms associated with insomnia when taken before bedtime.

Dill – also known as "church seed", can help to settle an upset tummy. Many years ago when church services would last most of the day, ladies would place dill seeds inside a folded handkerchief. These little seeds were then nibbled on during the long services, to freshen one's breath and calm a grumbly stomach. Once you plant dill you will never have to plant it again! Her seeds are many and her distribution is wide!

Garlic - better known as the "stinking rose" is an absolute staple in my kitchen. She is also crowned "nature's antibiotic" for her powerful antibacterial and antimicrobial properties. She not only adds a pungent flavor and aroma to many recipes and dishes, but, she can also increase the production of white blood cells in the body, which in turn may help to boost one's immune system.

Ginger Root - packs a real "zing" as well as being nicely warming and a superb antispasmodic. Ginger can help to relieve cramping associated with PMS, is an excellent anti-inflammatory, helps to ease motion sickness and nausea. Plus it is just plain tasty in many Asian dishes and other different recipes. Nothing can beat a lovely hot cup of ginger and lemon tea, sweetened with honey, to help settle an icky belly.

Mint - gives a jumpstart of green energy and is known as the "traveling" herb, for two reasons: (1) She will "travel" or spread far and wide in the herb garden. She can be very invasive, so if you do not want mint to take over your herb and/or flower beds, confine her to a container. (2) Mint mysteriously knows how to "travel" herself along with other medicinal companion herbs to the part of the body where it may be needed the most. Again, proof that herbs must be a God thing. Plus, she helps to make not so pleasant tasting herbs a bit more palatable. Mint is one of the largest species of herbs, with over 600 members. Most herbs with a square stem are considered to be part of the mint family. Talk about a lot of herbal cousins, wow!

---

*Of course with any new herb, herbal remedy, herbal supplement or herbal recipe, one should always consult their healthcare professional before trying, taking or using any new herb. I cannot stress the importance of proper herbal identification enough. When growing, harvesting or foraging for herbs if you are not 100% positive as to what you are using, just don't. Always remember, "when in doubt, leave it out!" *Julia Brown and/or A Simpler Thyme Ltd. is not a healthcare provider or facility.*

Rosemary - in the language of herbs and flowers rosemary is known as the herb of "remembrance". This is due to when you breathe in her wonderful aroma, it can give an uptake of oxygen to the brain, which may help to improve mental clarity, focus and awareness. Not to mention that some clinical studies have found her to be a great anti-inflammatory agent. Rosemary is steeped in folklore and traditions, making her one of my very favorite herbs and a must for my kitchen and herbal apothecary.

Sage - is known for her "wisdom" and "ancestral knowledge". Have you ever heard the old saying "take my sage advice", that's where this saying originated from. Sage isn't just for your thanksgiving bird, she is so much more flavorful and useful than only to be celebrated once a year. Her robust flavor can be enjoyed all year long and incorporated in many different recipes. Traditionally, sage is the go to herb for burning as incense or to smudge one's sacred space, to give purification and clarity. Sage does possess strong drying properties, so if pregnant or breastfeeding, limit your sage intake to a minimum.

Thyme - her leaves may be small, but she is a symbol of "courage". In ancient times, clear up until World War I and WWII, ladies would embroidery thyme and her flowers on handkerchiefs and give them to their beloved soldiers, before going into battle. As a reminder of their sacrifice, courage and bravery. I sometimes feel that thyme is often overlooked, as a delicious and beneficial herb. What she lacks for in size, she makes up for with a punch of lemony flavor. Thyme is another herb that helps to support the immune system, as well as having excellent anti-fungal and disinfectant properties to boot.

What is the difference between an herbal infusion and an herbal decoction?

Infusion

An infusion is when you take the flowers, leaves or stems of any said herb and pour boiling water over them. Allow them to steep for approximately 3-8 minutes to release the herbs' flavors and properties. Steeping some herbs for a longer period of time can cause them to taste bitter. Strain, then sweeten to taste with honey (never give honey to a child under the age of 2 years) or sweetener of choice. The average rule of thumb when making an herbal infusion or "cup of tea" is: 1 tsp. of herb or dried herbal blend - to 1 cup of hot water.

Decoction

A decoction is when you take the berries, bark or roots of any herb, place them in a pot or pan of cold water and bring the water up to a rolling boil. Once boiling, remove from heat, cover it with a lid and allow to steep for 8-15 minutes to release the herbs flavors and properties. Generally, when making a decoction, a longer steeping time is required to rehydrate the harder barks, berries or roots of herb. For example, cinnamon sticks, star anise, whole cloves, ginger root and dried citrus peels. Strain the decoction, then sweeten to taste with honey (never give honey to a child under the age of 2 years) or sweetener of choice.

Avocado Ice Cream with *Blueberry & Basil*

Into a food processor add the following:

2 ripe avocados halved
1 cup heavy cream
1 cup milk
1 cup fresh blueberries
1 tsp. fresh lemon juice
1 tsp. of lemon zest
½ cup powdered sugar
pinch of salt
1 small handful of fresh basil leaves (just eyeball it)

Blend on high until mixture is nice and smooth. If it appears too thick (depending on the size of the avocados) add more milk.

Transfer to a glass, freezer-safe dish with a lid. Freeze overnight until the ice cream is firm and set. Serve with a garnish of fresh blueberries and a sprig of basil.

Try switching things up with other fresh fruits and herbs: here are some suggestions:

Lemon Balm and Red Raspberries
Lavender and Blackberries
Lemon Verbena and Strawberries
Rosemary and Sour Pitted Cherries
Mint and Mango

I assure you, if you do not tell your guests or family that this ice cream is made from avocados… they will never be the wiser!

Herbal Fun Facts

Herbs have been used in many different ways since Biblical times, from culinary means, to medicinal and even spiritual practices. In Roman times, the herb thyme was believed to contain the powers of strength and courage if worn during war. Bay leaves were used to adorn the crowns of Olympic champions. In 18th century England, a stem of Rosemary was placed in a travelers shoe or coat pocket as a token of remembrance. If Lavender thrived in the garden, it was believed that the young lady of the house would never marry. In old world countries, a pot of basil was placed at the back door, to keep evil spirits from entering the home when strangers came calling.

Most culinary experts and chefs agree that fresh or dried herbs, when added to many different recipes and dishes, contribute to the overall flavor and appeal of the final dish; not to mention the nutritional properties contained in these God given herbs. Fresh or dried herb leaves are usually considered just that, an herb. However, the seeds of the herb plant are dubbed a spice. Basil is just one of my many favorites, basil with garlic, pine nuts and olive oil can easily be transformed into a wonderful pesto (recipe pg. 61) A stem of rosemary stripped of its lower leaves makes a super kabob skewer for grilled meats. Not only are herbs fragrant, delicious and lovely to look at, they can even help to rid your home of pests. Peppermint or spearmint plants grown near your home's foundation may help to deter mice and ants from entering. Who knew right!

Herbal Infused Ice Tea

Make ice tea as you normally would. I make sun tea in a glass gallon jar with a screw on lid, out on our back step.

Simply select a stem or two of your favorite herb and drop it into the tea jar. (You can use: mint, lemon balm, lavender, chamomile or any other herb of your liking)
Let the jar of tea steep on your back step for 8-10 hours in the sun. Remove tea bags and spent herbs. Sweeten if desired and serve over ice.

*Hint: freeze ice tea in your ice cube trays with a leaf of your herb of choice (or edible flower), this will keep your drink from becoming watered down as the "tea cubes" melt.

Herbal Sugar

To your food processor add ¼ cup of rinsed & completely pat dry fresh basil leaves or herb of choice, peppermint works nicely, and ½ cup of granulated sugar.

Pulse until combined to a granular consistency. Sprinkle over fresh fruit or add to a lovely cup of tea and enjoy. This will keep in an airtight container in the fridge for 1 week.

Herbal Infused Vinegar

Creating your own herbal infused vinegars is another way to bring your own creativity and unique flavor to your kitchen. Paring your favorite herbs with fresh fruits or aromatics, in a decorative bottle or jar, for your own use or for gift giving, can ignite your inner herbalist.

To a clean, quart jar, decorative bottle or repurposed wine bottle with a secure fitting lid, add the following:

Example #1
2-3 whole cloves of garlic
8-10 whole black peppercorns
1 whole chili pepper
1-2 sprigs of fresh rosemary

Example #2
2-3 sliced fresh strawberries
1-2 slices of lemon or orange peel
1-2 sprigs of fresh basil

Example #3
Everyone in the pool!
Try adding a sprig each of:
sage, thyme, rosemary & parsley
1-2 whole cloves of garlic

Example #4
8-10 fresh chive blossoms
This makes a lovely light purple colored vinegar

Fill the clean jar or bottle with apple cider vinegar. Set on your kitchen counter for up to 3-4 weeks, inverting the bottle once or twice a day to incorporate the contents and to give your loving intentions to your creation. After allotted time has expired, strain off the spent herbal content and rebottle for future use in salad dressings, marinades, stews, soups or stir fry. Also vinegar is an excellent meat tenderizer, try adding a couple tablespoons to your next pot roast for added flavor and tenderness.

sage

Edible Flowers

Adding edible flowers to desserts, salads, ice cubes, teas and more is a lovely way to bring the herb garden into your kitchen and enjoy their beauty and elegance. After all, I believe we "eat with our eyes first" so why not make your food beautiful!

Here are a few flowers that would be happy to adorn your plate:

- Basil Flowers
- Bee Balm
- Borage Flowers
- Calendula
- Chive Blossoms
- Dandelions
- Impatients
- Lavender Buds
- Mint Flowers
- Nasturtium
- Pansy
- Rose Petals
- Thyme Flowers
- Wild Violets

Egg-ucation - Which came first... the chicken or the egg?

    This is an age-old question that may never be answered. Eggs have been consumed by man since the beginning of time, including ostrich, quail, duck, goose, even turtle eggs and the more popular chicken egg that most of us enjoy today. In ancient Rome, the egg shell was crushed on the plate before eating to release evil spirits that were hiding inside the egg.

    Eggs contain and provide several vitamins and minerals and are one of the few foods that contain vitamin D along with vitamins A, B6, B12, iron, protein, potassium, calcium, folic acid and the list goes on. One large egg has approximately 75 calories and half of those are in the yolk. while the egg white contains no cholesterol and little, if any, fat. The color of the egg shell is caused by pigment deposits as the egg is forming. Generally chicken breeds with white ears lay white eggs and chickens with red ears lay brown eggs. However, there is no evidence of nutritional difference between the two. White eggs are thought of to be more mass and industrially produced, while most people prefer a fresh from the farm, cage free brown egg. So whether you like your eggs pickled, deviled or sunny side up, the goodness of a fresh egg can't be compared.

Egg & Fresh Herb Omelet

2 or 3 large fresh brown eggs
1 Tbsp. water
1 tsp. olive oil
1 Tbsp of butter
1 tsp. fresh chopped chives, dill weed & parsley (or herbs of your liking)

    In a medium bowl whisk eggs, water & oil together. In a small bowl combine fresh snipped herbs. Melt butter in a non-stick skillet, pour in egg mixture, cook until the bottom is golden brown, just before folding omelet in half sprinkle with half of the herb mixture. Fold and flip the omelet until golden on each side. Remove from the skillet and sprinkle with remaining herbs. Serve with fresh fruit and cheese if desired

Fresh Spinach & Spring Asparagus Quiche

INGREDIENTS:
½ cup half & half
1 cup fresh baby spinach
2 Tbsp. fresh chopped basil
¼ cup grated asiago cheese
8 - 10 large fresh brown eggs (depending on pan size)
1 package rolled refrigerated pie crust (or make your own)
¾ cup shredded sharp cheddar cheese
6 oz. fresh spring asparagus trimmed

Bring pie crust to room temp, place in a greased deep dish 9-inch pie plate. Preheat the oven to 350 degrees. Cut trimmed asparagus into 1 inch pieces, and blanch in salted boiling water for 2 - 4 minutes, drain - set aside. Sprinkle bottom of pie crust with basil, top with asiago cheese, spinach leaves, shredded cheddar and asparagus pieces. Beat eggs and cream together, salt and cracked black pepper to taste, pour over asparagus and cheese mixture. Bake for approx. 40 - 45 minutes or until the center is set or a knife blade inserted comes out clean. If necessary, cover the edge of the crust with foil to prevent over browning. Let the quiche stand for 10 - 15 minutes before cutting.

Zucchini Frittata
with *Mint & Basil*

4 tsp. olive oil (divided)
1 small zucchini diced
1 small purple onion chopped
1 clove crushed garlic
½ cup fresh cherry tomatoes halved
⅛ cup fresh mint slivered
⅛ cup fresh basil slivered
6 large brown eggs
2 Tbsp. milk
⅓ cup feta cheese
Salt & Pepper to taste

In a large oven-proof skillet (preferably cast iron) drizzle about 2 tsp. olive oil, over medium heat saute zucchini, garlic and onions until tender about 3 to 5 minutes. Add cherry tomatoes, herbs (reserve some for garnish), add salt & pepper to taste, cook until moisture has evaporated. In a large mixing bowl beat eggs and milk, to this add the hot zucchini mixture and feta cheese. Add the remaining 2 tsp olive oil to coat the pan evenly. Preheat the broiler. Return egg mixture to skillet on medium heat, without stirring, cook until light golden about 4 minutes, lift edges and tilt pan to let uncooked egg flow to the edges. Place skillet under broiler until frittata is set and top is golden approx. 2 - 3 minutes. Loosen edges and transfer to serving platter, cut into wedges, garnish with reserved herbs and serve.

Edible Salad Bowls

This is a very elegant way to serve a small mixed green salad. Your family and guests will be impressed at how lovely the presentation, but only you will know how simple and easy it was!

    To a hot non-stick pan, spread approximately ½ cup of shredded, parmesan cheese into an even circle shape. Let the cheese melt and start to turn golden brown, flip each side until equally golden. Remove from the pan and drape over a tall glass (a wine glass works great for this) and form into a bowl shape, allow to cool. As the cheese cools it will retain the bowl shape and crisp up. Remove from the glass and invert, now you have an edible salad bowl. Repeat the process until you have the desired amount of bowls needed. Fill with a nice spring mixed green salad, drizzle with salad dressing of choice and garnish with an edible flower. Trust me, your guests will be impressed!

Marinated "Dandy" Greens

This recipe is a great spring tonic. Dandelions are full of trace minerals and vitamins that our bodies crave after a long hard winter.

- 2 - 3 cups fresh tender dandelion greens - washed thoroughly and pat dry
- ½ cup Italian dressing (see pg. 86 for recipe)
- ¼ cup Raw honey
- Combine all ingredients and place in an airtight container in the fridge overnight. *This will pull out some of the bitterness from the greens.*

When ready to serve, drain off extra liquid and toss with ¼ cup feta or Parmesan cheese (whichever you prefer.) Top sourdough toast points with the marinated greens, place a slice of hard boiled egg on each, along with a bright yellow dandelion flower for garnish. Enjoy!

Fresh Spinach Salad with "a Lil Oink"

6 slices applewood smoked bacon (cooked crispy and drained well, let cool completely)
1 nice bunch of fresh tender spinach (washed thoroughly & pat dry)
½ cup fresh shelled peas (or frozen peas)
2 Tbsp. each of chopped fresh chives and Italian flat leaf parsley
¼ cup shredded Parmesan cheese
1 small bunch spring asparagus
3 hard boiled eggs chopped
Grated fresh nutmeg
Cracked Black Pepper to taste

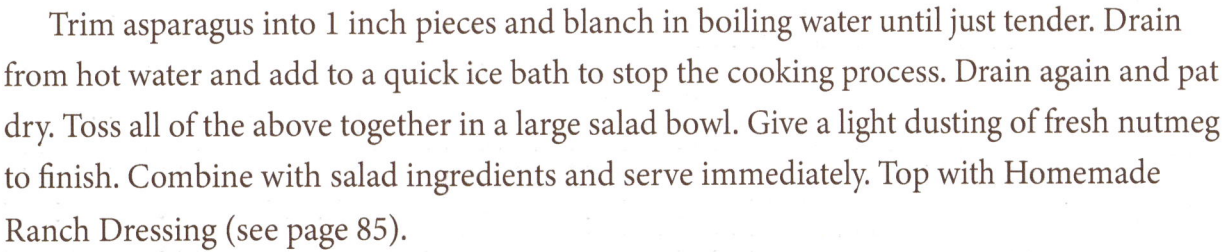

Trim asparagus into 1 inch pieces and blanch in boiling water until just tender. Drain from hot water and add to a quick ice bath to stop the cooking process. Drain again and pat dry. Toss all of the above together in a large salad bowl. Give a light dusting of fresh nutmeg to finish. Combine with salad ingredients and serve immediately. Top with Homemade Ranch Dressing (see page 85).

Lydia's Potato Soup with Dumplings

(My dear mother-in-law's recipe)

1-2 lbs. red skin potatoes with skins on - cut into bite size chunks

1 quart chicken stock (see pg. 64 or beef/veggie stock can be substituted)

1 medium sweet onion chopped

1 Tbsp. fresh chopped sage

1-2 cloves crushed garlic

3 Tbsp. olive oil

2 cups milk

2 Tbsp. butter

In a large Dutch oven saute onions and garlic in olive oil. Add stock, sage and potatoes, bring to a soft boil, reduce heat until potatoes are fork tender. Add milk and butter, bring back to a simmer.

Dumplings:

Mix together 1 cup of all purpose flour, 2 eggs and ¼ cup of ricotta cheese. Salt & pepper to taste. Combine until a coarse soft dough forms (if the dough feels too sticky, add a touch more flour). Add the dumplings by the teaspoonful into the simmering soup. Once the dumplings are in the pot, do not stir until the dumplings float. Remove pot from heat and allow the dumplings to continue to cook in the soup until set and cooked through.

sage

Warm Potato Salad with Springtime Herbs

- 1 bunch of fresh green onions cleaned & chopped *(including green tops)*
- 1 lb. small new & freshly dug spring potatoes *(halved)*
- ½ tsp. lemon zest plus 1 tbsp. lemon juice
- 2 tsp. fresh chopped flat leaf parsley
- 1 tsp. stone ground mustard
- 1 tsp. fresh chopped mint
- 1 tsp. honey *(or to taste)*
- 2 Tbsp. butter

In a medium pot bring potatoes to a boil in salted water, simmer for approx. 15-20 minutes; or until fork tender, drain. Transfer to a bowl and toss with butter, lemon zest & juice, mustard & honey, add onions, sprinkle with mint and parsley, toss gently, salt and black cracked pepper to taste, and serve warm. Garnish with a sprig of mint!

Potato - Potatoe

Did you know that the potato reached North American soil from England as early as 1585? Or that potatoes were once thought to be poisonous and had no place in the kitchen? This was because people tried eating the green tops, which are both very bitter and have poisonous toxins. I recommend not peeling your taters, the skin is where all the vitamins are. Lucky for us, our ancestors dug a little deeper for this kitchen staple and unearthed the spud!

BASIL PESTO

2 cups fresh basil leaves
3 - 4 whole cloves fresh garlic
1 lemon juice & zest
½ cup pine nuts or nut of choice *(almonds or walnuts work well)*
1 cup of Parmesan
Mix all ingredients in the food processor

Then add, with food processor running, extra virgin olive oil - until desired thickness is reached

Serve on pasta, grilled chicken, seafood, etc. Pesto freezes very well to enjoy that summertime flavor all winter long.

Pesto is such a lovely reminder of summertime freshness and the bounty of the herb garden. But, pesto can be enjoyed in a variety of ways, other herbs can be incorporated to give a different spin on this classic. Try switching out basil with one of the following herbs for a different twist:

Lemon Balm - wonderful with seafood or chicken
Sage - great with roasted poultry *very strong flavor*
Tarragon - pairs well with pork and beef
Rosemary & Mint - classic with roasted lamb

Or try a combination of herbs: cilantro, basil, chives, spinach or dandelion greens - let your creativity flow!

Mango Salsa

1 green pepper diced
1 sweet red pepper diced
1 large sweet purple onion chopped
3 medium red vine ripe tomatoes seeded & chopped
1 medium jalapeno pepper diced very small (seeds and membrane removed) more if you like it HOT!
8 oz can crushed pineapple drained (reserve juice)
1 medium sized ripe tropical mango diced (*Not to be confused with the Coshocton County mango... i.e. green pepper! If you know, you know! LOL*)
1-2 clove crushed garlic
2-3 Tbsp. fresh chopped cilantro
1 Tbsp. fresh chopped flat leaf parsley
1 Tbsp. fresh chopped basil
¼ cup apple cider vinegar
2 tbsp. honey
Zest and juice of 1 small lime
Salt & pepper to taste

In a large bowl combine the first 11 ingredients. Into reserved pineapple juice, whisk: vinegar, honey, lime juice & zest, salt & pepper. Combine with veggie and Mango mixture. Place in an airtight container and refrigerate until chilled, serve with corn chips or crackers. This salsa is also great alongside grilled chicken or pork and will keep in the fridge for up to 1 week.

basil

Mickey's (My Mamma's) Spaghetti Sauce

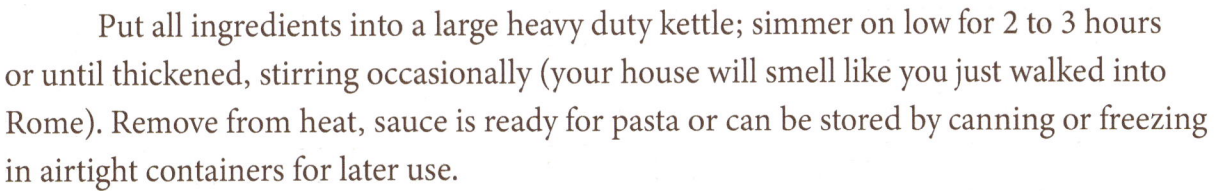

- 1 qt. tomato juice
- 1 Tbsp. kosher salt
- 1 Tbsp. dried basil
- ¼ cup sugar
- 2 Tbsp. dried parsley flakes
- 1 Tbsp. dried oregano
- 32 oz. crushed tomatoes
- 3 - 4 cloves crushed garlic

Put all ingredients into a large heavy duty kettle; simmer on low for 2 to 3 hours or until thickened, stirring occasionally (your house will smell like you just walked into Rome). Remove from heat, sauce is ready for pasta or can be stored by canning or freezing in airtight containers for later use.

Mother's Meatballs

- 1 lb. lean ground beef (80/20)
- 1 lb. Italian sausage
- 1 cup seasoned Italian bread crumbs
- ½ cup grated parmesan cheese
- 1 Tbsp. Worcestershire sauce
- 2 - 3 cloves finely minced garlic
- 1 small onion finely minced
- 2 eggs
- 1 tsp. dried basil
- 1 tsp. dried parsley
- ½ tsp. dried oregano
- Salt & black cracked pepper to taste

Mix all of the above in a large bowl until well combined. Shape into large meatballs (approximately 6) Place onto a rimmed baking sheet lined with aluminum foil. Bake off at 350 degrees until no longer pink in the center or until juices run clear, turning to brown on all sides, approx. 40 minutes or until desired doneness. Once baked, transfer meatballs into a simmering pot of spaghetti sauce. Heat on low until sauce is warmed through, ready to serve over pasta or with a nice crusty loaf of Italian bread. Garnish with fresh basil and a sprinkling of grated parmesan cheese, enjoy with a glass of your favorite red wine. Highly recommended!

Around the World Tomatoes

    Take several large, off the vine ripe tomatoes or mix it up with a variety of colorful heirloom tomatoes, wash and pat dry. Slice into perfect rounds, then try adding some of the following condiments to travel the globe. Layer a platter with tomatoes slices and top each slice with some of the following flavors:

Mediterranean - a dab of minced garlic, feta cheese, chopped fresh parsley and basil, lemon zest.

Tex-Mex - a dab of minced garlic, chopped cilantro, lime zest and a slice of pickled jalapeno.

Asian - a dab of minced ginger root, thin slices of purple onion, chopped cilantro, rice wine vinegar.

Italian - a dab of minced garlic, chopped fresh basil and oregano, olive oil, sliced black olives.

Season all with salt and black cracked pepper to taste.

Classic Caprese Salad

Simply slice up several large ripe tomatoes (you can use different heirloom varieties), layer each tomato slice between a slice of fresh buffalo mozzarella cheese and freshly picked basil leaves on a large platter. Drizzle with extra virgin olive oil, balsamic vinegar and salt & pepper to taste. Simple, beautiful and delicious!

BASIL WAFERS

2 Tbsp. of fresh chopped basil
1 tsp. lemon zest
1 cup parmesan

Mix together the ingredients in a small bowl. Spoon onto a parchment-lined baking sheet and form into small rounds. Bake 400° for 5-8 minutes until crisp & golden. Move to a cooling rack, allow wafers to cool completely. Serve with salad or dip.

basil

History behind the Midwest Mango - Green Pepper Confusion

Back in the colonial era, getting local mangoes wasn't an option so they had to import them. Due to the lack of refrigeration they began pickling the mango, as well as many other fruits, especially green peppers (commonly thought to be a vegetable). As a result, the word 'mango' took on a new identity and turned into a verb, meaning "to pickle," and thus the midwest mango began.

Stuffed Pepper (Mango) Soup

1 lb. ground beef
4 - 5 large green peppers chopped
1 large onion diced
2 - 3 cloves crushed garlic minced
2 tsp. dried parsley
Salt & Pepper to taste
1 quart of tomato juice
1 pint of diced stewed tomatoes - do not drain
1 quart of beef stock
1 box Uncle Ben's long grain brown rice with season packet
2 Tbsp. Worcestershire sauce
Chopped fresh parsley for garnish

In a large Dutch oven brown ground beef with peppers, onions, garlic and dried parsley until onions and peppers are tender and beef is no longer pink. Add the remaining ingredients, simmer on medium heat until rice is cooked and tender. Garnish with fresh parsley and serve with a good crusty bread, along with a nice compound butter (page 61).

VEGETABLE LASAGNA

2 or 3 yellow summer squashes (cut lengthwise) or 2 large patty pan squash

1 bunch of rainbow Swiss chard (washed, trimmed & chopped)

1 sweet onion chopped

1 red sweet pepper sliced in rings

1 green pepper sliced in rings

1 or 2 cloves of crushed garlic

1 lb. Italian sausage

1 package shredded mozzarella cheese (approximately 2 cups)

16 oz. spaghetti sauce (see pg. 30)

Salt & pepper to taste

Fresh chopped basil

Cook sausage, garlic and onions together and drain excess fat, stir in sauce and heat through. In a greased 9x13 baking dish, layer squash, Swiss chard, pepper rings, sausage mixture and cheese (about 3 layers - finishing with cheese on top). Bake at 350 degrees for about 40 minutes or until veggies are tender and cheese is golden brown. Remove from the oven. Allow to set and cool slightly before cutting to serve, sprinkle with the chopped basil to garnish. Delicious and nutritious.

There are no noodles in this dish, the squash acts as and takes the place of the noodles - this recipe is great for anyone that needs to eat Gluten Free.

Grilled Corn
with
Lime Butter

Soak a dozen fresh ears of corn in the husks in a sink full of cold water, for about an hour.

Remove husks and place on a hot grill for approximately 15 to 20 minutes depending on the temperature of the grill.

When corn is steamed to perfection, mix up the following:

1 stick of butter at room temp
Juice of 1 fresh lime
Zest of the lime
2 Tbsp. of fresh chopped cilantro
1 tsp. chili powder
Mix all of the above together into a nice smooth butter, then slather on fresh grilled corn.
Salt & Pepper to taste.
Sprinkle with crumbled feta or queso fresco cheese - if desired.

Fresh Corn Chowder

8 ears of sweet corn - cut from the cob
4 medium newly dug potatoes - diced
1 can of cream corn
1 medium candy/sweet onion - chopped
1 to 2 cloves crushed garlic minced
32 oz. chicken stock (see pg. 63)
1 large chicken breast cooked & chopped
1 cup heavy cream
2 Tbsp. butter
1 Tbsp. each fresh chopped parsley, sage & rosemary
Salt & pepper to taste

    In a large Dutch oven sauté onions & garlic in a little olive oil until lightly browned, add potatoes, corn, chicken stock and chicken breast pieces - simmer on medium heat until potatoes are fork tender. Add cream, butter and herbs, bring back up to a simmer, add salt and black cracked pepper to taste.

Garden Folk Lore

It is said that "one is closer to God in the garden, than any place else on earth." As a Master Herbalist, this certainly resonates with me. There is just something uniquely special and spiritually connecting, about being in touch with nature, while working in or just admiring my herb gardens. So let's share some "Garden Folk Lore" to spark your interest and green thumbs. Did you know that in Ireland the Lily of the Valley is also known as fairy ladders, for the "wee-folk" to climb. Also, another legend says that these tiny white flowers came from the tears that Mary shed at the foot of the cross, when Christ was crucified.

You should consider planting mint in your garden, although it can be invasive, it is a must for the backyard kitchen garden. In 17th century lore it was believed that if mint flourished in your herb garden, it was said to bring money or coins to your purse. Speaking of money, it was once believed that if you found a spider crawling on your clothes, you would soon come into wealth. Spiders were also used as weather forecasters. When a storm is approaching a spider will tighten its web, when fair skies are about to return the spider will let out the threads again. So, remember this old saying "If you wish to live and thrive, let the spider stay alive".

Shepherds Pie with an *Herbal Flare*

1 lb. ground lamb
1 leek chopped *(washed thoroughly of all dirt and sand)*
1 medium onion chopped
2 - 3 cloves crushed garlic minced
½ tsp. dried rosemary
½ tsp. dried thyme
½ tsp. dried mint
2 or 3 medium sized red potatoes chopped *(remember to leave the skins on - that's where the vitamins live)*
Dollop of sour cream
1 Tbsp. of butter
Splash of milk
1 small bag of frozen mixed veggies *(about 2 cups worth)*
½ tsp. fresh chopped rosemary
½ tsp. fresh chopped thyme
½ tsp. fresh chopped mint
2 pie crusts *(one for the top and one for the bottom)*
2 Tbsp. corn starch
Salt & Pepper to taste
1 egg & 2 Tbsp. water *(to make egg wash for the top pie crust.)*

    This is a truly delicious old Irish classic, with an herbal spin on it! In a large cast iron skillet brown ground lamb with onions, leeks, garlic and dried herbs. Add a bit of olive oil, (lamb tends to be rather on the lean side) and salt & pepper to taste, cook until onions and leeks are tender and lamb is no longer pink. Set aside. Preheat the oven to 350 degrees. In a pan of salted boiling water, cook potatoes until fork tender, drain well, add sour cream, butter & milk. Give a rough mash to the potatoes. To the skillet add: frozen veggies, fresh chopped herbs and corn starch, salt and pepper, mix well. Spread mashed potatoes into the bottom of your deep dish prepared pie crust, pour lamb & veggie mixture over top of the potatoes, arrange evenly, cover with top crust, cut a few vent holes in the top crust to allow the steam to escape while baking. Beat egg with water, mix together and brush over the top crust, so it comes out of the oven a beautiful golden brown color. Bake at 350 degrees for approximately 30 - 40 minutes or until mixture is heated through and has thickened up. Allow to cool and set up some before serving.

Homemade Ketchup

6 lbs. fresh tomatoes (about 18 medium)
1 cup red wine vinegar
2 tsp. Worcestershire sauce
1 (6 oz.) can tomato paste
3 - 4 cloves crushed garlic

1½ cup brown sugar
½ tsp. chili powder
½ tsp. grated ginger
1 tsp. salt
1 tsp. pepper

    Wash tomatoes, cut out cores, remove skins and seeds, crush tomatoes one layer at a time with an old potato masher. In a large kettle bring crushed tomatoes to a soft boil, stirring often. Reduce heat and simmer for about 30 minutes.
    Combine tomatoes, paste and vinegar, bring back to boil, stir frequently. Slowly add sugar and remaining ingredients to the kettle until evenly incorporated. Reduce heat and simmer for 10 more minutes. Ketchup is ready! Makes approximately 5 pints. Process in sterile jars, give hot bath or place in freezer safe containers and freeze for future use.

RED, WHITE, & BLUE BURGERS

1 Tbsp. dried Italian herb blend (basil, oregano, parsley, rosemary, red hot pepper flakes)
3 lbs. lean ground beef (Makes 8 burgers)
One envelope Lipton onion soup mix
1 clove crushed garlic
Several large ripe tomatoes sliced

Cheese Mixture:
1 (3oz.) package cream cheese, softened
½ cup crumbled blue cheese, softened

    In a large mixing bowl combine ground beef, garlic, and herb blend, add 2 Tbsp. onion soup mix. Mix well and divide into 8 portions. In a medium bowl, combine blue cheese, cream cheese and remaining soup mix. Divide into 8 portions.

    Place a spoonful of the cheese mixture on top of each portion of beef shaping beef around the cheese to form 8 balls. Flatten into patties approximately ¾ inch thick, refrigerate for at least 1 hour before cooking. Grill burgers until cooked through, serve on toasted buns with a thick slice of tomato.

Rustic Strawberry Tart

INGREDIENTS:

1 prepared pie dough to form a 12 inch pie

1 quart of fresh strawberries sliced

1 Tbsp. fresh chopped basil

1 Tbsp. fresh chopped mint (a pineapple mint works lovely)

1 Tbsp. water (add a little more if puree seems too thick)

¼ cup honey

¼ cup brown sugar

4 Tbsp. graham cracker crumbs

1 Tbsp. melted butter

2 tsp. Sugar

    In a medium saucepan place half of the strawberries, water, honey and brown sugar. Bring to a soft boil over medium heat, cook stirring often until thickened puree forms. Transfer puree to bowl and let cool to room temperature. Preheat the oven to 400 degrees. Line the baking sheet with parchment paper, place a 12 inch pie crust on paper. Leaving a 2 inch border of dough, sprinkle graham cracker crumbs in the center of the crust, spread puree over crumbs leaving the 2" inch border untouched, toss the fresh basil & mint with the remaining fresh berries and place on top of the puree.

    Shape the tart by folding the untouched edges toward the center, pleating as necessary to form a 9 inch tart. Brush outer edges with melted butter and sprinkle with sugar. Reduce the oven to 350 degrees and bake for 35 - 40 minutes or until the crust is golden brown and the filling is bubbling. Allow to cool completely, garnish with fresh basil & mint before serving.

Good Morning Smoothie

INGREDIENTS:

1½ cup of whole milk, coconut or almond milk

Small handful of fresh mint or lemon balm leaves

1 cup fresh sliced strawberries

1 banana cut into chunks

¼ cup orange juice

½ tsp. vanilla

1 inch nice chunk of fresh ginger root peeled

Pinch of cinnamon

Sweeten with honey to taste if desired

Put all of the above into a blender, cover and blend for approximately 1 - 2 minutes or well incorporated. Pour into glasses and garnish with an orange slice and whole strawberry, you can add a mint leaf too if desired. Enjoy!

Ratatouille

2 medium onions sliced thin
3 - 4 cloves crushed garlic
¼ cup olive oil
2 small zucchini cut into ½ inch slices
3 ripe tomatoes diced

1 medium eggplant peeled & cubed into 1 inch pieces
2 tsp. chopped fresh parsley
1 Tbsp. chopped fresh oregano
1 Tbsp. chopped fresh basil
Salt & Pepper to taste

In a large Dutch oven, sauté onions and garlic in olive oil until onions are translucent, add remaining veggies, simmer until vegetables are tender and juices have thickened, approximately 15 - 20 minutes. Add fresh herbs at the end to retain their brightness and flavor. Remove from heat and toss. For an added bonus sprinkle with freshly grated parmesan cheese and garnish with fresh basil leaves.

Too Hot to Cook Salad

Clean and slice 2 large Portabella mushroom caps and a large fennel bulb (save fennel fronds for garnish). Arrange mushroom and fennel slices on a platter, drizzle with extra virgin olive oil and balsamic vinegar, salt and pepper to taste, sprinkle with chopped fennel fronds.

This simple salad is great with a loaf of fresh homemade bread and compound butter (recipe see pg. 61). A few fresh juicy peaches sliced in a bowl with whipped cream, and a glass of your favorite white wine. Just saying!

Asparagus Roll-Ups

One nice bunch of fresh tender asparagus, ends trimmed
1 lb. medium sliced turkey breast deli lunch meat
1 lb. thin sliced provolone cheese
Basil pesto (see pg. 28)

Blanch asparagus in boiling salted water for approximately 4 - 5 minutes. Remove from hot water and immediately cold shock in ice bath to stop the cooking process. Drain well and pat dry with paper towels.

On a clean flat work surface:

Layer 1 slice of turkey, on top of that 1 slice of cheese, spread with a butter knife a thin amount of basil pesto over the cheese. Place 1 spear of asparagus at the edge of the meat & cheese and roll it up. Move to a decorative serving platter, repeat the process until you have used up all the asparagus stems. Arrange roll ups on the platter, drizzle with a good balsamic vinegar if desired and garnish with fresh basil leaves. Serve or chill for later. Cheese is best at room temperature.

Garden Pasta Salad

1 (16 oz.) box whole wheat penne pasta (cook according to package directions & drain)

½ cup olive oil

¼ cup red wine vinegar

1-2 Tbsp. sugar (to taste)

1 tsp. stone ground mustard

1-2 cloves crushed garlic minced

2 tsp. each of fresh chopped parsley & basil

Salt & black cracked pepper to taste

1 cups cherry tomatoes, halved

1 cup diced cucumber

1 small diced yellow summer squash

1 red sweet pepper chopped

1 small sweet onion diced

½ cup sliced black olives

½ cup shredded parmesan cheese

    In a small bowl whisk oil, vinegar, sugar, salt & pepper, mustard, garlic and herbs together. Into a large bowl combine remaining ingredients, toss with dressing. Ready to serve. I prefer this salad at room temperature, rather than chilled first, but certainly delicious either way. Refrigerate any leftovers.

Grandma Edna's Pickled Veggies

2 cups sweet red and green peppers cut into strips
1 small head cauliflower broken into florets
2 cups peel carrots cut into 1" slices
4 cups cucumbers cut into 1" slices
2 cups sliced sweet onion
4 quarts water
1 cup salt

6 cups apple cider vinegar
3 cups water
2 cups sugar
¼ cup mustard seeds
2 Tbsp. celery seeds
12 crushed garlic cloves (more if desired)

Dissolve 1 cup of salt into 4 quarts of water, pour over mixed veggies in a very large bowl, let stand overnight covered with a clean kitchen towel in a cool place, drain well. Combine spices, sugar, vinegar & water in a large kettle, bring to boil for 3 minutes. Pack mixed veggies into hot sterile jars, pour in boiling liquid & spices and give jars a 20 minute hot water bath. Remove from the hot water bath, place them on a towel on your counter until completely cooled and the lids have sealed. Listen for the "pop" of each jar.

Dilly Beans

2 - 3 lbs. fresh trimmed green beans (leave whole)
6 small red hot chili peppers (optional)
1 large onion sliced into 6 rounds
60 black whole peppercorns
3 tsp. whole mustard seeds
6 seed heads of fresh dill
6 whole garlic cloves

1 cup sugar
3 cups water
1 Tbsp. kosher salt
6 cups apple cider vinegar

Sterilize 6 wide mouth canning jars, lids and rings. Bring vinegar, water, sugar & salt to boil over medium heat until sugar and salt are completely dissolved. Meanwhile into each wide mouth jar put 1 garlic clove, ½ tsp. mustard seeds, 10 black peppercorns and pack each jar with fresh green beans, 1 dill head, 1 chili pepper, and 1 slice of onion. Pour liquid over beans until it reaches the rim of the jar. Secure lids and give hot water bath, until jars are sealed for about 20 minutes. Remove from the hot water bath, place them on a towel on your counter until completely cooled and the lids have sealed. Listen for the "pop" of each jar.

Depression Vinegar Pie

One 9" pie shell
4 large brown eggs
¾ cup sugar
¼ cup honey
3 Tbsp. flour
¼ cup flavored herbal vinegar (such as mint - see page 15)
6 Tbsp. melted butter
Whipped cream and fresh fruit for garnish

    Line the pie shell with parchment paper, then put in beans, rice or pie weights, this old trick is called "blind baking." This technique helps to ensure the crust stays crisp, once the liquid filling is added. Bake for 10 minutes at 450 degrees, then remove weights and paper. Return the pie shell to the oven, reduce heat to 350 degrees and bake for another 8 minutes or until a light golden brown, remove and let cool. In a bowl beat eggs until smooth and a lemon yellow color. Add sugar, honey, vinegar and flour, beat well, then mix in butter slowly. Pour into the pie shell and bake at 350 degrees for 25 minutes or until filling is set. Let cool, serve with whipped topping and sliced fresh fruit.

Food for Thought...

If our forefathers taught us anything, it was to utilize all things that are made available to us. You know the old saying "waste not want not," this tradition should still ring true today. We have all become so accustomed to speed and convenience in our food and its preparation, maybe it's time to rethink our food choices, as well as our selections and get back to basics? If it worked 100 years ago, chances are it will still work today. Plus when food is crafted with love and made with the resources that are given us, the end result is far more satisfying. My Mother always said "a good cook uses what she or he has on hand and rarely measures anything (just eyeball it). You cook with instinct and trust your gut, if you like it and make it with love, your family will like it too."

A couple great tips to help build that cooked all day depth of flavor are: always sweat down your aromatics (garlic, peppers & onions) in a good quality olive oil. It's okay to skimp on some pantry items, but the price of a good quality olive oil will pay for itself once it hits the table. When you are using dried herbs, add them at the beginning of whatever it is that you are preparing, this will give the dried herbs time to rehydrate and release their vital oils, flavors and properties. When cooking with fresh herbs add them in at the end of the cooking process to retain their vibrant color, flavor and properties. Think "less is more" when using dried herbs, because their flavors are intensified during the drying process. Think the opposite when using fresh herbs, it's okay to use a "heavy hand", because the vital oils of the herb have not been concentrated in the drying process yet.

Let's Get to the "Core" with a Little Apple History

The ever so popular apple became the symbol of knowledge and of sin in the story of Adam and Eve. In Latin the words for apple and evil are very similar. Even our larynx or "Adams Apple" is derived to have come from the forbidden fruit sticking in Adams' throat, when he took that infamous first bite. In Greek mythology, the goddess Eris, angered and jealous that she wasn't invited to a wedding, tossed a golden apple inscribed (Most Beautiful) into the wedding party. The Greek goddess of Love - Aphrodite was awarded this apple. She then in turn tempted Paris of Troy with the most beautiful woman in all the world, which Greek legends held as Helen of Sparta. He awarded the golden apple back to Aphrodite, thus indirectly beginning the Trojan War. Like they say "all because of a woman!"

The old proverb "an apple a day keeps the doctor away" may very well have some ring of truth to it. Not only are apples a great source of fiber, but they lead the way in vitamin C, E, B6, and minerals such as potassium, calcium, magnesium, plus many antioxidants compared to other fruits. Apples are as American, as well … apple pie! An estimated 93 million tons of apples are grown and produced worldwide every year.

OLD FASHIONED Apple Crisp

INGREDIENTS:

¼ tsp. ground clove
1 tsp. cinnamon
½ tsp. nutmeg
½ tsp. salt
4 cups sliced apples
½ cup butter, softened
⅓ cup brown sugar
1 cup oatmeal

Layer apples in an 8" square deep dish baking pan. Sprinkle apples with spices and salt. Work together in a separate bowl: sugar, oatmeal and butter until crumbly. Spread crumble mixture over apples. Bake at 350 degrees for about 30 - 40 minutes or until the apples are tender. Serve with whipped topping, vanilla ice cream or milk.

Classic Apple Salad with an *Herbal Twist*

Apple Mixture:
1 Fuji apple, diced
1 Red Gala apple, diced
1 Granny Smith apple, diced
½ cup thinly sliced celery
½ cup chopped walnuts
¼ cup golden raisins
½ cup crumbled goat cheese (feta will work too)
Fresh spring greens or baby spinach leaves

Dressing:
1 cloves crushed garlic
1 Tbsp. grated onion
1 cup mayo
2 Tbsp. red wine vinegar
2 Tbsp. milk
1 Tbsp. local honey (or to taste)
1 tsp. fresh chopped thyme
1 tsp. fresh rosemary
Salt and black cracked pepper to taste

In a large bowl, mix together apples, celery, cheese, nuts and raisins. In a separate bowl combine dressing ingredients, mix well. Pour dressing over the apple mixture and toss well. Serve apple salad on a bed on mixed greens. Serve immediately. Garish with fresh herbs and celery leaves if desired.

Pumpkin Soup
a "Harvest Hug" in a Bowl!

1 medium onion diced
2 cloves minced garlic
1 tsp. dried sage
½ tsp. dried thyme
1 tsp. dried rosemary

3 - 4 Tbsp. olive oil
3 cups chicken stock (see pg. 63)
½ cup heavy cream
2 - 3 pats of butter

1 (30 oz.) can of pumpkin puree (be sure to NOT pick up pumpkin pie mix! Way too sweet!)

In a Dutch oven saute onions, garlic and dried herbs in olive oil, until the onions are translucent. Add pumpkin puree and chicken stock, bring to a low simmer. Add cream and butter, salt and black cracked pepper to taste, bring back up to a low simmer. Ladle hot soup into bowls, garnish with roasted pumpkin seeds and fresh ribbons of sage.

Harvest Blessings The word harvest is derived from the Anglo-Saxon word "haerfest" which translated means "autumn" (my favorite time of year and our daughters name). The once celebrated holiday (Lammas) on August 1st also known as "Loaf Day" was an early harvest celebration of the first gathering of autumn wheat. Local communities would bake loaves of bread made from this first wheat cutting and give to local churches for communion, to show their thanks and gratitude for a good harvest. Of course one's thoughts turn to the widely celebrated holiday of Thanksgiving (Turkey Day) as a national day of thanks. However, not only was the first Thanksgiving a celebration of the harvest, but a union of family and community as well. It was and still is a time to be grateful for nature's bounty and abundance to our tables.

Personally, for me, there is just something about making homemade soup on a cold winter's day that is very therapeutic. I don't know if it is the chopping of the veggies and herbs or making a bone broth from scratch, or the wonderful aroma that engulfs the entire house. But, soup on a cold day warms the body, mind and soul. Maybe it's the steam rising up from the bowl, as you blow on that first spoonful. Or feeling the warmth as it travels over your tongue and down your throat, as it warms your chest. Or that a large kettle of soup is just made for sharing with others, over a loaf of crusty bread and a pot of herbal tea. Regardless of the reasons, hot homemade soup is like a friendly hug from the inside out!

DUTCH HARVEST CHILI

2 lbs. Italian sausage

1 large onion, chopped

2 - 3 crushed garlic cloves

2 medium sweet red peppers, chopped

1 - 2 large sweet potatoes, cut into 1 inch cubes

1 can black beans, drained and rinsed

1 can of white hominy, drained (yellow corn can be substituted)

1 (32 oz.) can crushed tomatoes

1 small can chopped green chili peppers

1 bottle stout-dark beer

1 quart of chicken stock (see pg. 63)

2 medium granny smith apples, peeled, cored and chopped

Salt and black cracked pepper to taste

Sour cream

Shredded cheddar cheese

Fresh chopped cilantro

    In a large Dutch oven, brown sausage, onions and garlic until sausage is no longer pink and onions are tender. Add peppers and sweet potatoes and stir well. Cook over medium heat for another five minutes or so, but do not allow the sweet potatoes to burn. Add remaining ingredients, bring to a boil, then reduce heat and simmer for 30 minutes covered or until sweet potatoes are fork tender. Serve with a dollop of sour cream, cheese and cilantro on top. This chili has a rich dark color and, like most chili, is better the next day.

Jack-O-Lanterns have been associated with Halloween since Civil War times. Folklore suggests that it was once believed that the cutout holes of Jack's face were used as portholes by demons to come in and out. If set outside of the home these vessels would prevent evil spirits from entering and exiting through the windows and doors of one's dwelling, thus keeping the house ghost free on All-Hallows-Eve. The name Jack comes from an Irish legend, that a mean, nasty and greedy old man named Jack, tricked the devil into climbing up a tall tree. Jack then carved a cross at the bottom of the tree trunk so the devil couldn't climb back down. In revenge, the devil placed an evil curse on Jack, condemning him to forever wander the earth each night with only a lit candle placed inside a hollowed out turnip. American's later incorporated the pumpkin in place of the turnip, which was easier to carve. And hence, the ever popular Jack-o-lantern was born.

Dinner in a Pumpkin

This is a fun way to get the whole family involved in meal prep and a unique way to serve dinner.

Select a nice round medium size pumpkin, cut off the top to form a lid and scoop out seeds (set aside to roast later if desired) and pulp. The pumpkin will be your cooking and serving vessel for this one "pot" meal. In a skillet, brown 1 lb. zesty Italian sausage, one small onion chopped and 2-3 cloves of crushed garlic until sausage is no longer pink and onions are tender.

Add to the pumpkin the following:

Sausage mixture
1 tsp. dried parsley
½ tsp. dried rosemary
8 oz. fresh sliced mushrooms
1 (8 oz.) can cream of mushroom soup
8 oz. can sliced & drained water chestnuts
1 box Uncle Ben's quick cooking long grain wild rice with season packet - prepared by box directions

2 - 3 carrots sliced into coins
1 (8 oz.) can corn - drained
¼ cup brown sugar
2 Tbsp. soy sauce
Salt & pepper to taste

Mix all of the above inside of the pumpkin, top with lid. Place pumpkin on a rimmed baking sheet. Bake at 350 degrees for approx. 1 hour or until pumpkin flesh is tender. Serve into bowls directly from the pumpkin.

French Toast Bake

1 loaf of a good French or Sourdough bread - cubed
8 fresh brown eggs
2 cups milk
2 cups half-and-half
2 tsp. vanilla
½ tsp. nutmeg
½ tsp. cinnamon
¼ tsp. ground clove
¾ cup melted butter
1 cup brown sugar
2 Tbsp. maple syrup
1 cup chopped pecans or walnuts

Cut bread into 1 inch pieces and place in a well buttered 9x13 baking dish. Beat eggs, milk, half-and-half and spices together pour over bread and refrigerate overnight. In the morning make the topping by mixing butter, brown sugar, maple syrup and pecans together. Spread evenly over top of egg mixture, bake at 350 degrees for about 40 - 50 minutes. Place the baking dish on a cookie sheet while baking in-case of boiling over. Serve with fresh mixed berries alongside, with an extra drizzle of maple

Overnight Oatmeal

Generously butter the inside of a slow cooker or crock pot.

To this add the following ingredients:

¼ cup brown sugar

2 Tbsp. melted butter

¼ tsp. salt

½ tsp. cinnamon

½ tsp. nutmeg

1 cup quick cooking oats

1 medium apple peeled, cored and diced

½ cup raisins or dried cranberries (or try a ¼ cup of each)

½ cup chopped walnuts or pecans

4 ½ cups milk

    Place all of the above into the well greased slow cooker; mix well. Set on low heat overnight, about 6 - 8 hrs; spoon into bowls to serve, garnish with fresh blueberries and a drizzle of honey. It's a great way to start a chilly morning!

Compound Butter

INGREDIENTS:
1 cup room temperature natural butter (2 sticks)
1 Tbsp. fresh lemon juice
1 tsp. fresh lemon zest
1 clove crushed garlic minced
¼ cup of fresh chopped herb or combination of herbs - *make sure herbs are washed and pat very dry, you don't want to add extra moisture to your butter*
Salt & Black Cracked Pepper to taste

In a medium bowl mix well until all ingredients are combined, form into a ball. Move to a large piece of plastic wrap, shape into a log. Cover with the plastic wrap, refrigerate until firm, about 1 hour. Remove and use on bread, pasta, veggies or melt a medallion of compound butter on top of a perfectly grilled ribeye steak or thick cut pork chop... delicious!

Here are some suggestions of herbal combinations for compound butter, but feel free to use your own herbal creativity.

Dill & Parsley
Sage & Lovage
Basil & Oregano
Rosemary & Thyme
Chives - *use stems and the lovely purple chive flowers*

HOMEMADE CHICKEN STOCK/BROTH

A good stock / broth is incredibly nourishing to the body, not to mention the immense depth of flavor it adds to your dish. The marrow contained inside of the bones is nutrient dense in trace minerals. Plus, added bonus, your house will smell out of this world, while it simmers away on the stovetop. This may seem like a lot of effort, rather than just opening a box of stock from the store (not that there's anything wrong with that, in a pinch), but trust me you will taste the difference. The end result is worth the time and effort!

INGREDIENTS:

1 whole chicken carcass roasted and picked of most of the meat - *this can be leftover from Sunday dinner or you are perfectly allowed to cheat and use a rotisserie chicken from the supermarket. No one will judge, especially if you don't tell them!*

1 large onion quartered - leave peel on to give a rich amber color to the broth

5 - 6 cloves whole garlic

2 - 3 ribs of celery - rough cut into chunks

1 apple quartered

1 lemon halved

2 large carrots rough cut into chunks - do not peel, that is where the vitamins are!

2 each nice healthy sprigs of the following herbs: sage, thyme, rosemary, parsley

2 - 3 bay leaves

1 tsp. whole black peppercorns

Salt to taste - a good Celtic sea salt is excellent for this stock.

Place all of the above in a large kettle, top with 8 - 10 quarts of water, depending on the size of your pot. Simmer on low heat for 3 - 4 hours, stirring occasionally. Remove from heat and let it sit, until the contents have come to room temperature. Strain off broth, store broth in an airtight container in the fridge or pour into freezer bags and freeze for later use.

If you are wanting to make a beef broth rather than chicken, place beef bones from the butcher, on a sheet tray, drizzle with olive oil, sprinkle with salt and pepper. Roast off in the oven (about 1 hour at 350 degrees). Then simply repeat the above and you will have an excellent rich beef broth instead of chicken.

Lemon Chicken Orzo Soup

1 ½ cups cooked chicken breast - cubed
2 quarts chicken stock (see pg. 63)
1 cup orzo pasta
1 medium onion diced
3 - 4 cloves garlic finely minced
3 Tbsp. olive oil
Juice and zest of 1 lemon
¼ cup fresh chopped flat leaf parsley
Salt & cracked black pepper to taste

    In a large Dutch oven saute onions and garlic in olive oil until onions are tender. Add stock and bring up to a low simmer, add orzo, simmer until orzo starts to become tender. Add chicken, lemon juice and zest, continue on a low simmer until pasta is done. Stir the fresh parsley in at the very end just before serving, season with salt and pepper to taste. Serve with a loaf of crusty bread and a nice compound butter. (see pg. 61)

Jalapeno Cornbread

3 cups cornbread mix (like Jiffy)
2 cups buttermilk
¼ cup vegetable oil
¼ cup red sweet pepper chopped fine
6 slices of bacon (cooked & crumbled)
1 ½ cup shredded Mexican blend cheese
¼ cup finely chopped jalapeno peppers (seeds and membranes removed)
1 small onion grated
1 cup cream style corn
2 Tbsp. sugar
1 clove crushed garlic
3 fresh brown eggs beaten

    Combine cornbread mix and milk in a large bowl. Add remaining ingredients, mix well, pour into a greased 9x13 pan, bake at 350 degrees for approximately 40 minutes or until a knife inserted comes out clean. This bread is great with soup beans or chili.

Turkey/Game Day Cranberry Relish

This is not your grandma's cranberry sauce! The beauty of this twist on a classic, is that you can enjoy it plain alongside your bird or dress it up for game day tailgaters!

INGREDIENTS:

1 (14 oz.) can whole cranberry sauce (Ocean Spray)
½ cup sugar
Juice & zest of 1 lime
1 clove crushed and finely minced garlic
1 small purple onion finely diced
1 large jalapeno (seeds & membrane removed) finely diced
½ cup of chopped cilantro

In a saucepan on low heat dissolve sugar in cranberry sauce. Remove from heat, set aside and allow to come to room temperature. Meanwhile, finely dice the aromatics, place in a serving bowl with cilantro, lime juice and zest. Once cranberries are cooled, mix with the other ingredients. Ready to enjoy, alongside your turkey day bird or with crackers.

To fancy this cranberry sauce up as an appetizer: simply spread a package of softened cream cheese on a serving platter, cover with a layer of the cranberry mixture. Serve with crackers or corn chips, garnish with fresh cilantro leaves. Yum!

This is a family tradition for the holidays & birthdays

In a large mixing bowl combine all but the chocolate chips. Mix on high with an electric mixer until all is combined, then gently fold in chocolate chips. Transfer to a well greased and floured Bundt pan. Bake at 350 degrees for 40-45 minutes or until a knife inserted comes out clean. Allow to cool completely before inverting the cake from the pan, to a cake stand or platter. Dust lightly with powdered sugar. Serve with whipped topping if desired, garnish with fresh mint or rosemary.

INGREDIENTS:
- 1 (15 oz.) box devil's food cake mix
- 1 cup of cold strong black coffee
- 1 (4 oz.) box instant chocolate pudding
- ½ cup dark spiced rum
- 1 (11.5 oz.) bag chocolate chips
- ½ cup sour cream
- ¼ tsp. cinnamon
- 1 tsp. vanilla
- Pinch of salt
- 4 eggs

Christmas, the most "Wonderful" time of the year.

Hanging stockings by the fire with care is a favorite in most every household on Christmas Eve. Legend has it that 3 poor sisters had no dowry for their wedding day. One of the sisters had hung her wet woolen sock by the hearth to dry. Father Christmas had heard of these poor girls' dilemma and threw 3 bags of gold coins down the chimney, one for each girl. The third bag landed in the sock hung to dry! That is why Santa still gives children chocolate gold wrapped coins to this day.

We all know that a wreath hung on one's front door is a sign of welcome. But a holly wreath hung, not only welcomes your guests, but is a reminder of the reason for the season. The points on the holly leaves represent the thorns worn by Christ and the red holly berries symbolize His blood. The popular colors of red and green that are used throughout the Christmas season have their own meaning as well. Green stands for a promise of rebirth and life, red once again stands for the blood of Christ.

People young and old alike always enjoy getting caught under the mistletoe. This legend comes from the Scandinavian goddess Frigga, whose son was shot with an arrow made of mistletoe wood. Her tears became the white berries and she ordered that mistletoe would never be used to harm anyone ever again. Instead it would be a symbol of love and everyone that passed under it, the beautiful goddess would kiss.

Celebration Rum Cake

Cranberry & Rosemary Chicken Salad

½ cup dried cranberries

2 ribs of celery diced

¼ cup chopped walnuts

1 small sweet onion diced

2 - 3 large chicken breasts - grilled/cooked - cut into bite size pieces

Combine all of the above in a mixing bowl, set aside.

Dressing:

1 cup mayo

2 Tbsp. of rosemary infused vinegar (see pg. 15)

2 tsp. finely chopped fresh rosemary

1 clove crushed garlic minced

Juice of 1 small lemon

2 Tbsp. sugar

Splash of milk if dressing appears too thick

Salt & Black Cracked Pepper to taste

Blend the above together in a small bowl.

    Pour dressing over chicken mixture, toss to incorporate, ensuring all is coated nicely. Serve as a sandwich on a bagel or croissant. Or place on a bed of fresh greens alongside sliced melon or pears, garnish with a small spring of fresh rosemary. Refrigerate any leftovers.

Baked Pears with Cranberry Sauce

4 - 6 large ripe Bartlett pears (peeled, cut in half & cored)
1 can of whole cranberry sauce
1 cup sugar
1 tsp. vanilla
¼ tsp. cinnamon
Dash of nutmeg
Pinch of salt
1 - 2 sprigs of fresh rosemary
⅓ cup chopped walnuts

    Place pear halves cut side up in a lightly greased baking dish. Meanwhile in a small saucepan heat cranberry sauce, sugar, salt, vanilla, rosemary, cinnamon & nutmeg together until heated through and sugar is completely dissolved. Pour over pears, sprinkle with walnuts. Bake at 350 degrees for approx. 20 - 30 minutes or until pears are hot and sauce is bubbly. Dish up two pears & generous amount of sauce per plate and serve with a scoop of vanilla bean ice cream, garnish with a sprig of fresh mint. One word YUMMY!

Layered Pear & Blue Cheese Tower

4 perfectly ripe pears - cut into slices lengthwise
Crumbled blue cheese
Walnuts
Honey
Fresh arugula
Salt & Black Cracked Pepper to taste

    On a bed of fresh arugula build your tower by layering pear slices, cheese crumbles and walnut pieces. Drizzle with honey and season to taste with salt and pepper. This simple salad is not only delicious, but extremely elegant. Makes four towers.

HOT MULLED WASSAIL

1 gallon fresh apple cider
2 cups cranberry juice
1 cup orange juice
1 cup sugar
2 - 3 Star Anise
6 whole cinnamon sticks
Spike one small orange with whole cloves

Put all of the above into a nice size kettle or pot, heat on a low simmer until nicely warmed through, stirring until sugar is completely dissolved. Serve in mugs, garnish with cinnamon sticks if desired. Not only does this recipe taste great, it will make your entire kitchen smell like a winter wonderland *You could also make an adult version of this by adding a bottle of red wine, in place of the cranberry and orange juices.*

Homemade Hot Cocoa

2 chocolate bars chopped
2 cups half-and-half
2 white chocolate bars chopped
8 cups whole milk
1 Tbsp. pure vanilla
½ tsp. ground cardamom
½ tsp. cinnamon
Pinch of cayenne pepper
Pinch of salt

In a large kettle or Dutch oven, combine half-and-half with chocolate over medium heat, whisk constantly until chocolate is melted. Add milk, vanilla and spices, whisking until combined. Bring to a simmer but do not boil. Ladle into mugs; Garnish with whipped cream, crushed candy canes and shaved chocolate (if desired).

Drop Herb Biscuits

1 egg
¼ cup milk
2 tsp. olive oil
2 cups Bisquick
1 crushed clove of garlic
½ cup shredded cheese of your choice
Chopped fresh herbs of choice (*chives, basil, parsley, sage, rosemary, dill weed, oregano... let your inner herbalist run wild... whatever culinary herb you fancy!*)
Salt & pepper to taste

Mix all of the above until a light dough forms, drop large spoonfuls onto a greased baking sheet. Bake at 350 degrees for approximately 12-15 minutes or until golden brown and center is set. Serve warm with compound butter. (see pg. 61)

Christmas Honey & Thyme Cookies

1 cup butter softened (2 sticks)

¼ cup local honey (or maple syrup can be substituted)

2 tsp. pure vanilla extract

2 cups flour

1 cups chopped walnuts or pecans

1 Tbsp. fresh chopped thyme

½ tsp. salt

In a large bowl mix butter on high speed until creamy, add honey and vanilla beat until smooth. With the mixer on low speed, mix in flour, walnuts, thyme and salt until dough forms. Cover bowl with plastic wrap and chill for one hour. Preheat the oven to 325 degrees. With lightly floured hands shape dough into 1 inch balls. Place on a non-stick cookie sheet, press floured fork across top of each ball to make decorative indentation. Bake for 15 - 18 minutes or until golden brown.

Grandma Edna's Spiced *Christmas Beets*

My grandmother's pickled beet recipe. She'll probably be turning over in her grave that I'm sharing it... but here goes nothing. Love you Grandma!

INGREDIENTS:

3 - 5 lbs. fresh baby spring beets
2 cups apple cider vinegar
2 cups water
2 cups sugar
1 tsp. kosher salt
1 tsp. ground allspice
6 cinnamon sticks
12 whole cloves
6 thin lemon slices

Bring beets to boil until fork tender, drain and peel skins. Cut into chunks and place in 6 sterilized canning jars. Bring the vinegar, water, sugar, salt and allspice to a rolling boil. Pour over beets; add one cinnamon stick, 2 cloves and a lemon slice to each jar. Seal jars with a hot water bath, as normal. (Grandma called these her "Christmas Beets' because everyone always got a jar as part of their Christmas gift.)

Steak Florentine

INGREDIENTS:

2 lbs. top round sirloin pounded out to approximately ½ inch thick
2 - 3 Tbsp. Italian dressing (see pg 85)
10 oz. of fresh tender spinach, washed well, pat dry, and chopped fine
1 small chopped sweet onion
¼ cup sweet red pepper diced fine
1 - 2 cloves crushed garlic minced
2 tsp. each fresh basil & oregano leaves chopped fine
2 Tbsp. grated Romano cheese
2 Tbsp. grated Parmesan cheese
1 (14 oz.) can diced tomatoes

Cut steak into 2 pieces, each about 10x4 inches. Place steak on a clean cutting board and brush with dressing. In a medium bowl combine: spinach, onion, garlic, basil and cheeses; mix well. Stir in one cup of tomatoes. Spoon one cup of mixture over each steak, spreading to cover the steak evenly. Roll up steak, jelly-roll fashion, tie rolls with butcher's string. Place rolls in a 9x13 oven safe pan and pour remaining spinach mixture and tomatoes over the meat. Cover with foil, bake at 350 degrees for approximately 1 hour or until meat is done and tender.

Spiced Winter Roasted Vegetables

4 - 6 large parsnips, scrubbed and trimmed

4 - 6 carrots scrubbed and trimmed (leave peel on both the above)

2 large beets - skin removed

1 - 2 cups trimmed & halved fresh brussel sprouts

1 sweet onion quartered

1 purple onion quartered

6 - 8 garlic cloves left whole (more if you're a garlic lover, like me)

6 - 8 Tbsp. olive oil

½ tsp. chili powder

¼ tsp. smoked paprika

Pinch of cinnamon

Salt and black cracked pepper to taste

Fresh chopped parsley

Shredded parmesan cheese

Preheat the oven to 425 degrees. Cut parsnips, carrots & beets into wedges of similar size. On an oven safe sheet pan, spread veggies out evenly, drizzle with olive oil and sprinkle with spices. Toss to coat. Reduce heat to 350 degrees and roast for approx. 35 - 40 minutes, toss occasionally, until root veggies are tender. Sprinkle with Parmesan cheese and fresh chopped parsley to garnish.

Root Vegetables: Traditionally speaking, there is a reason why certain crops of vegetables come to harvest at a particular season. Take root veggies for instance, most root vegetables are trace mineral dense. Why? Where do root veggies mature? In the earth, right! That is exactly where most trace minerals are found. During the long cold months of winter, our bodies need those trace minerals to sustain and nourish us until spring. Much like the old Kodiak bear, we need those vitamin and mineral dense foods to "winter us over" as we hibernate, waiting to emerge after a long winter's rest. It is amazing to me, how our great Provider has each food perfectly timed to each season, to supply all of our needs.

Chicken Root Stew

INGREDIENTS:

3 Tbsp. olive oil

16 ounces fresh dark green kale or spinach (rinsed, pat dry & chopped)

2 quarts of chicken stock (see pg. 63)

3 bay leaves

2 red sweet peppers chopped

3 sprigs each: fresh thyme, rosemary, sage and parsley (tied together with cooking string - for easy removal later)

1 large sweet onion chopped

3 - 4 crushed garlic cloves

2 cups diced red potatoes

2 cups diced carrots

1 cup peeled and chopped turnips

1 cup chopped fennel bulb (save frons for garnish)

1 cup peeled and chopped parsnips

1 small head of cabbage chopped

1 can chickpeas (drained and rinsed)

2 or 3 cups cooked chicken breasts

Salt and pepper to taste

    In a large Dutch oven, heat olive oil and saute kale, garlic and onions. Add ½ cup of the broth, stir often and cover cook for about 5 minutes. Or until greens are softened, do not allow greens to burn. Add all remaining ingredients, simmer for about 30 minutes or until the veggies are tender. Remove bay leaves and herb sprigs. Add salt and pepper to taste. Garnish with shredded cheddar cheese and chopped fresh herbs if desired.

Easy - "Peasy" Salad

1 lb. of frozen peas
1 cup shredded cheddar cheese
1 small purple onion - diced
6 - 8 pieces of bacon - crispy, crumbed & cooled
Salt & pepper to taste

Mix all the above in a large bowl.

Dressing:
½ cup Milk
½ cup Mayo
2 Tbsp. Sugar (to taste)
2 Tbsp. Red Wine Vinegar
Salt & pepper to taste

Blend all the above in a small bowl. Pour over pea mixture and toss to coat evenly. This salad is great to set out on a buffet, because the frozen peas will keep the salad chilled as they thaw.

Poorman's Salmon Dinner

This meal was a staple in my mothers' arsenal of kitchen favorites. It is now one of my family's go-to comfort meals. These salmon patties are moist, tender, flaky and full of flavor! This meal is not complete without mashed potatoes and sweet green peas with butter. Yum! It takes me back home every time I prepare it!

1 can of Pink Alaskan Caught Salmon - drained well and cartilage removed
1 sleeve of round butter crackers - crushed
2 eggs
1 Tbsp. dried dill weed
1 Tbsp. fresh chopped chives
1 tsp. onion powder
½ tsp. garlic powder
Black cracked pepper to taste
(No real reason to add salt - the cracker will provide the saltiness)

Mix all of the above together and form nice sized patties. Brown salmon patties in a non-stick skillet with a drizzle of olive oil, until golden on both sides. Makes 4 patties. Serve with mashed potatoes and peas!

Open Faced Rustic Plum Tart

1 9" pie crust
¼ cup apricot jam
2 Tbsp. fresh chopped mint
6-8 fresh plums cut into wedges
1 large fresh brown egg & 1 Tbsp. water - whisked together for egg wash
½ cup raw sugar

Line a baking sheet with parchment, unfold pie crust onto the pan, spread with jam and sprinkle with mint, leaving a 2 inch border around the edge. Arrange plums on top of jam and mint. Fold edges of crust over leaving the center exposed and press lightly to seal. Brush outside edges of pie dough with egg wash and sprinkle with raw sugar. Bake at 350 degrees for about 30 - 40 minutes or until cooked through and golden. Serve warm with vanilla bean ice cream, garnish with fresh mint. Note * this tart would be just as delicious using fresh pears instead*

Forget-Us-Not

Traditionally, on Valentine's Day, very long ago it was not the rose that was given by young men to their sweethearts, but rather the pansy and the forget-me-not. The pansy symbolizes love and kind thoughts, whereas the forget-me-not means friendship, fidelity and remembrance. In old English folklore it was once said that an angel fell in love with a mortal woman and was banished from heaven. The angel could only return to heaven if they both planted forget-me-nots in every corner of the universe. The angel and his lover worked relentlessly, until St. Peter took pity on the two and allowed them both back into heaven once again. Ensuring that true love never fails!

Stuffed Dates

This treat is a true labor of love, but so worth the effort, your Valentine will be thrilled by your outpouring of thoughtfulness.

INGREDIENTS:

3 Packages of pitted large dates
1 lb. thick sliced bacon
1 lb. zesty Italian sausage or can substitute ground turkey
2 shallots minced
1-2 cloves crushed garlic minced
1 tsp. dried basil
¼ tsp. hot red pepper flakes (more if brave)

    Into a skillet add sausage, shallots, garlic, basil and pepper flakes. Cook sausage until no longer pink, drain off all fat, allow to cool. Combine cooled sausage with one 8 oz. package of cream cheese, mix well. Stuff each date with sausage & cream cheese mixture. Cut each bacon slice into thirds, wrap each date with a piece of bacon. Place wrapped dates into a 9x13 pan, Bake at 350 degrees for approximately 30 minutes, or until bacon is done and slightly crispy. Remove with a slotted spoon from the pan, place on paper towels to absorb excess bacon fat, then arrange on a serving platter. Serve warm.

Dressings

Homemade Ranch

1 cup buttermilk
½ cup sour cream
2 Tbsp. apple cider vinegar
1 tsp. onion powder
1 tsp. garlic powder
½ tsp. paprika
½ tsp dried parsley
½ tsp. dried basil
½ tsp. dried thyme
2-3 Tbsp. Sugar - to taste

Place all the above in a mason jar, shake well. Ready to use. Refrigerate any unused amounts.

Ginger Citrus

¼ cup red wine vinegar
½ cup extra virgin olive oil
1 crushed garlic clove
Juice of 1 lemon or orange (Or try half of each)
1 inch chunk of fresh grated ginger (More for a kick)
3-4 Tbsp of honey (to taste)
Salt & Black Cracked Pepper to taste

Place all the above in a mason jar, shake well. Ready to use. Refrigerate any unused amounts.

Apple Thyme

½ cup olive oil
½ tsp. onion powder
1-2 crushed cloves garlic
¼ cup apple cider vinegar
2 Tbsp. fresh chopped Thyme
Juice & zest of 1 small lemon
2-3 Tbsp. honey - to taste
Salt & Pepper - to taste

Place all the above in a mason jar, shake well. Ready to use. Refrigerate any unused amounts.

Italian

½ cup olive oil
¼ cup red wine vinegar
1-2 cloves crushed garlic
1 tsp. onion powder
¼ tsp. red pepper flakes
Lemon juice & zest of 1 small lemon
2 Tbsp. honey - to taste
Salt & Black Cracked Pepper to taste

½ tsp. of the following dried herbs:
Basil
Oregano
Rosemary
Parsley
Thyme

Place all the above in a mason jar, shake well. Ready to use. Refrigerate any unused amounts.

Waste Not, Want Not

½ cup olive oil
¼ cup of herbal vinegar (see pg. 15)
1 Tbsp. honey - to taste

Place oil and vinegar in an almost empty jam or jelly jar (strawberry, raspberry, apple and black current are all tasty options) shake well. Ready to use. Refrigerate any unused amounts.

Creamy Garlic

1 clove crushed garlic
1 Tbsp, grated onion
1 cup mayo
2 Tbsp. red wine vinegar
2 Tbsp. milk
1 Tbsp local honey (or to taste)
1 tsp each of fresh chopped thyme & rosemary
Salt and black cracked pepper to taste

Place all the above in a mason jar, shake well. Ready to use. Refrigerate any unused amounts.

Three Sisters

    As the old Native American legend tells, we are all sisters by nature. Perhaps not by blood, but connected just the same. Each woman caring for, nourishing, uplifting, loving and providing for the other. Regardless of age, social status, education, wealth or fame. But simply showing compassion, respect and kindness... one women to another. As the old legend suggests, 3 sisters were left alone to fend for themselves, all of them loving the other more than herself. The oldest sister being straight and tall in stature, had long golden hair and a beautiful smile. The middle sister being wild and always running, stretching her imagination like vines to great lengths. The youngest sister being small and rather roundish, keeping herself grounded and hidden beneath her older sisters. All 3 of them worked together, each using her own skills, talents and strengths to achieve and provide for their needs. To this day, in some Native American cultures they still plant corn (the oldest sister), pole beans (the middle sister) and pumpkins or squash (the younger sister) together. The corn provides the beans her stalk to climb, as the beans anchor the corn so she does not blow over in high winds. While the pumpkin uses her big wide leaves to shade the corn stalks and the beans' roots from the hot summer sun and provides natural mulch. Again, all 3 working, supporting and nourishing one another.

    As Olivia, Amy and myself came together to collaborate on "A Simpler Thyme in the Kitchen" I was reminded of this old story. The 3 of us, using our God given skills, talents and strengths to bring this cookbook of ancestral knowledge, wisdom and recipes to life. I extend my humble thanks and appreciation, to my two sisters (not by blood) but by choice, for their efforts and skill sets that made this dream a reality.

Olivia Stock Julia Brown Amy Casey

Cooking Conversions

Index

A

Apples
Apple History	51
Apple Thyme Salad Dressing	85
Classic Apple Salad with an Herbal Twist	52
Dutch Harvest Chili	55
Homemade Chicken Stock	63
Old Fashioned Apple Crisp	51
Overnight Oatmeal	60

Apricot
Open Faced Rustic Plum Tart	83

Arugula
Layered Pear & Blue Cheese Towers	72

Asparagus
Asparagus Roll-Ups	44
Fresh Spinach & Spring Asparagus Quiche	19
Fresh Spinach Salad with "a Lil Oink"	22

Avocado
Avocado - Blueberry & Basil Ice Cream	12

B

Bay Leaves
Chicken Root Stew	80
Herbal Fun Facts	13
Homemade Chicken Stock	63

Bacon
Easy - "Peasy" Salad	81
Fresh Spinach Salad with "a Lil Oink"	22
Jalapeno Cornbread	65
Stuffed Dates	84

Basil, Dried
Homemade Ranch Dressing	85
Italian Dressing	86
Mickey's Spaghetti Sauce	30
Mother's Meatballs	30
Red, White and Blue Burger	40
Stuffed Dates	84

Basil, Fresh
Around the World Tomatoes	31
Asparagus Roll-Ups	44
Avocado - Blueberry & Basil Ice Cream	12
Basil Wafers	32
Classic Basil Pesto	28
Classic Caprese Salad	32
Compound Butter	61
Drop Herb Biscuits	75
Edible Flowers	16
Fresh Spinach & Spring Asparagus Quiche	19
Garden Pasta Salad	45
Herbal Fun Facts	13
Herbal Sugar	14
Herbal Vinegar	15
Herbs and their Beneficial Properties	5
Mango Salsa	29
Ratatouille	43
Rustic Strawberry Tart	41
Steak Florentine	78
Vegetable Lasagna	34
Zucchini Frittata with Mint & Basil	20

Beans
Depression Vinegar Pie	47
Dilly Beans	46
Dutch Harvest Chili	55

Three Sisters	87

Beef
Mother's Meatballs	30
Red, White and Blue Burgers	40
Stuffed Pepper (Mango) Soup	33

Beets
Grandma Edna's Spiced Beets	77
Spiced Winter Roasted Vegetables	79

Blueberries
Avocado - Blueberry & Basil Ice Cream	12
Overnight Oatmeal	60

Broth/Stock
Chicken Root Stew	80
Dutch Harvest Chili	55
Fresh Corn Chowder	36
Homemade Chicken Stock	63
Lemon Chicken Orzo Soup	65
Lydia's Potato Soup w/Dumplings	23
Pumpkin Soup - A "Harvest Hug"	53
Stuffed Pepper (Mango) Soup	33

C

Carrots
Chicken Root Stew	80
Dinner in a Pumpkin	58
Grandma Edna's Pickled Veggies	46
Homemade Chicken Stock	63
Spiced Winter Roasted Vegetables	79

Celery
Classic Apple Salad w/an Herbal Twist	52
Cranberry - Rosemary Chicken Salad	71
Homemade Chicken Stock	63

Chicken
Chicken Root Stew	80
Cranberry - Rosemary Chicken Salad	71
Eggucation	17
Fresh Corn Chowder	36
Homemade Chicken Stock	63
Lemon Chicken Orzo Soup	65

Chives
Egg & Fresh Herb Omelet	18
Classic Basil Pesto	28
Compound Butter	61
Drop Herb Biscuits	75
Fresh Spinach Salad with "a Lil Oink"	22
Poorman's Salmon Dinner	82

Cilantro
Around the World Tomatoes	31
Classic Basil Pesto	28
Dutch Harvest Chili	55
Grilled Corn with Lime Butter	35
Mango Salsa	29
Turkey/Game Day Cranberry Relish	66

Cinnamon
Baked Pears with Cranberry Sauce	72
Celebration Rum Cake	69
French Toast Bake	59
Good Morning Smoothie	42
Grandma Edna's Spiced Christmas Beets	77
Homemade Hot Cocoa	75
Hot Mulled Wassail	74
Old Fashioned Apple Crisp	51
Overnight Oatmeal	60
Spiced Winter Roasted Vegetables	79

Clove

Difference Between Infusion & decoction 8
French Toast Bake 59
Grandma Edna's Spiced Christmas Beets 77
Hot Mulled Wassail 74
Old Fashioned Apple Crisp 51

Corn
Dinner In A Pumpkin 58
Dutch Harvest Chili 55
Fresh Corn Chowder 36
Grilled Corn with Lime Butter 35
Jalapeno Cornbread 65
Three Sisters 87

Cranberries
Baked Pears with Cranberry Sauce 72
Cranberry - Rosemary Chicken Salad 71
Hot Mulled Wassail 74
Overnight Oatmeal 60
Turkey/Game Day Cranberry Relish 66

Cucumbers
Garden Pasta Salad 45
Grandma Edna's Pickled Veggies 46

D

Dandelions
Classic Basil Pesto 28
Edible Flowers 16
Marinated "Dandy" Greens 22

Dill Weed
Compound Butter 61
Dilly Beans 46
Drop Herb Biscuits 75
Egg & Fresh Herb Omelet 18
Herbs and their Beneficial Properties 5
Marinated "Dandy" Greens 22
Poorman's Salmon Dinner 82

E

Eggs
Celebration Rum Cake 69
Depression Vinegar Pie 47
Drop Herb Biscuits 75
Egg & Fresh Herb Omelet 18
Eggucation 17
French Toast Bake 59
Fresh Spinach & Spring Asparagus Quiche 19
Fresh Spinach Salad with "a Lil Oink" 22
Jalapeno Cornbread 65
Lydia's Potato Soup w/Dumplings 23
Marinated "Dandy" Greens 22
Mother's Meatballs 30
Open Faced Rustic Plum Tart 83
Poorman's Salmon Dinner 82
Shepard's Pie with an Herbal Flare 38
Zucchini Frittata with Mint & Basil 20

F

Fennel
Too Hot to Cook Salad 43
Chicken Root Stew 80

G

Garlic
Apple Thyme Salad Dressing 85
Around the World Tomatoes 31
Chicken Root Stew 80
Classic Apple Salad w/an Herbal Twist 52

Classic Basil Pesto	28
Compound Butter	61
Cranberry - Rosemary Chicken Salad	71
Dilly Beans	46
Drop Herb Biscuits	75
Dutch Harvest Chili	55
Fresh Corn Chowder	36
Garden Pasta Salad	45
Ginger Citrus Dressing	85
Grandma Edna's Pickled Veggies	46
Herbal Infused Vinegar	15
Herbs and their Beneficial Properties	5
Homemade Chicken Stock	63
Homemade Ketchup	39
Italian Dressing	86
Jalapeno Cornbread	65
Lemon Chicken Orzo Soup	65
Lydia's Potato Soup w/Dumplings	23
Mango Salsa	29
Mickey's Spaghetti Sauce	30
Mother's Meatballs	30
Pumpkin Soup - A "Harvest Hug"	53
Ratatouille	43
Red, White and Blue Burgers	40
Shepard's Pie with an Herbal Flare	38
Spiced Winter Roasted Vegetables	79
Steak Florentine	78
Stuffed Pepper (Mango) Soup	33

Ginger

Around the World Tomatoes	31
Difference Between Infusion & Decoction	8
Ginger Citrus Dressing	85
Good Morning Smoothie	42
Herbs and their Beneficial Properties	5
Homemade Ketchup	39

H

Honey

Apple Thyme Salad Dressing	85
Christmas Honey-Thyme Cookies	76
Classic Apple Salad with an Herbal Twist	52
Depression Vinegar Pie	47
Difference Between Infusion & Decoction	8
Ginger Citrus Dressing	85
Good Morning Smoothie	42
Herbs and their Beneficial Properties	5
Italian Dressing	86
Layered Pear & Blue Cheese Towers	72
Mango Salsa	29
Marinated "Dandy" Greens	22
Overnight Oatmeal	60
Rustic Strawberry Tart	41
Warm Potato Salad w/Springtime Herbs	24

L

Lemon

Apple Thyme Salad Dressing	85
Around the World Tomatoes	31
Avocado - Blueberry & Basil Ice Cream	12
Basil Wafers	32
Classic Basil Pesto	28
Compound Butter	61
Cranberry - Rosemary Chicken Salad	71
Ginger Citrus Dressing	85

Grandma Edna's Spiced Christmas Beets	77
Herbal Infused Vinegar	15
Homemade Chicken Stock	63
Italian Dressing	86
Lemon Chicken Orzo Soup	65
Warm Potato Salad w/Springtime Herbs	24

Lemon Balm

Avocado - Blueberry & Basil Ice Cream	12
Classic Basil Pesto	28
Good Morning Smoothie	42
Herbal Infused Ice Tea	14

Lime

Around the World Tomatoes	31
Grilled Corn with Lime Butter	35
Mango Salsa	29
Turkey/Game Day Cranberry Relish	66

M

Mango

Avocado - Blueberry & Basil Ice Cream	12
Mango Salsa	29

Mint

Avocado - Blueberry & Basil Ice Cream	12
Baked Pears with Cranberry Sauce	72
Celebration Rum Cake	69
Classic Basil Pesto	28
Edible Flowers	16
Garden Folk Lore	37
Good Morning Smoothie	42
Herbal Fun Facts	13
Herbal Infused Ice Tea	14
Herbal Sugar	14
Herbs and their Beneficial Properties	5

Open Faced Rustic Plum Tart	83
Rustic Strawberry Tart	41
Shepard's Pie with an Herbal Flare	38
Warm Potato Salad w/Springtime Herbs	24
Zucchini Frittata with Mint & Basil	20

N

Nutmeg

Baked Pears with Cranberry Sauce	72
French Toast Bake	59
Fresh Spinach Salad with "a Lil Oink"	22
Old Fashioned Apple Crisp	51
Overnight Oatmeal	60

Nuts

Christmas Honey-Thyme Cookies	76
Classic Apple Salad w/Herbal Twist	52
Classic Basil Pesto	28
Cranberry - Rosemary Chicken Salad	71
French Toast Bake	59
Layered Pear & Blue Cheese Towers	72
Overnight Oatmeal	60

O

Olives

Around the World Tomatoes	31
Garden Pasta Salad	45

Onion

Around the World Tomatoes	31
Chicken Root Stew	80
Classic Apple Salad w/Herbal Twist	52
Cranberry - Rosemary Chicken Salad	71
Dilly Beans	46
Dinner in a Pumpkin	58

Dutch Harvest Chili — 55
Easy - "Peasy" Salad — 81
Fresh Corn Chowder — 36
Garden Pasta Salad — 45
Grandma Edna's Pickled Veggies — 46
Homemade Chicken Stock — 63
Jalapeno Cornbread — 65
Lemon Chicken Orzo Soup — 65
Lydia's Potato Soup w/Dumplings — 23
Mango Salsa — 29
Mother's Meatballs — 30
Pumpkin Soup - A "Harvest Hug" — 53
Ratatouille — 43
Shepard's Pie with an Herbal Flare — 38
Spiced Winter Roasted Vegetables — 79
Steak Florentine — 78
Stuffed Pepper (Mango) Soup — 33
Vegetable Lasagna — 34
Warm Potato Salad w/Spring Herbs — 24
Zucchini Frittata with Mint & Basil — 20

Orange
Ginger Citrus Dressing — 85
Good Morning Smoothie — 42
Herbal Infused Vinegar — 15
Hot Mulled Cider or Wassail — 74

Oregano
Around the World Tomatoes — 31
Compound Butter — 61
Drop Herb Biscuits — 75
Italian Dressing — 86
Mickey's Spaghetti Sauce — 30
Mother's Meatballs — 30
Ratatouille — 43
Red, White and Blue Burgers — 40
Steak Florentine — 78

P

Parsley
Around the World Tomatoes — 31
Chicken Root Stew — 80
Compound Butter — 61
Creamy Ranch Dressing — 85
Dinner In A Pumpkin — 58
Drop Herb Biscuits — 75
Egg & Fresh Herb Omelet — 18
Fresh Corn Chowder — 36
Fresh Spinach Salad w/ "a Lil Oink" — 22
Garden Pasta Salad — 45
Herbal Infused Vinegar — 15
Homemade Chicken Stock — 63
Italian Dressing — 86
Lemon Chicken Orzo Soup — 65
Mango Salsa — 29
Mickey's Spaghetti Sauce — 30
Mother's Meatballs — 30
Ratatouille — 43
Red, White and Blue Burgers — 40
Spiced Winter Roasted Vegetables — 79
Stuffed Pepper (Mango) Soup — 33
Warm Potato Salad w/Spring Herbs — 24

Parsnips
Chicken Root Stew — 80
Spiced Winter Roasted Vegetables — 79

Pears
Baked Pears with Cranberry Sauce — 72
Layered Pear & Blue Cheese Towers — 72

Peas

Easy - "Peasy" Salad	81
Fresh Spinach Salad with "a Lil Oink"	22
Poorman's Salmon Dinner	82

Peppers

Chicken Root Stew	80
Dilly Beans	46
Dutch Harvest Chili	55
Grandma Edna's Pickled Veggies	46
Jalapeno Cornbread	65
Stuffed Pepper (Mango) Soup	33

Potatos

Chicken Root Stew	80
Dutch Harvest Chili	55
Fresh Corn Chowder	36
Lydia's Potato Soup w/Dumplings	23
Poorman's Salmon Dinner	82
Shepard's Pie with an Herbal Flare	38
Warm Potato Salad w/Spring Herbs	24

Pumpkin

Dinner In A Pumpkin	58
Pumpkin Soup - A "Harvest Hug"	53
Three Sisters	87

R

Rosemary

Avocado - Blueberry & Basil Ice Cream	12
Baked Pears with Cranberry Sauce	72
Chicken Root Stew	80
Classic Apple Salad w/an Herbal Twist	52
Classic Basil Pesto	28
Compound Butter	61
Cranberry - Rosemary Chicken Salad	71
Dinner in a Pumpkin	58
Drop Herb Biscuits	75
Fresh Corn Chowder	36
Herbal Fun Facts	13
Herbal Infused Vinegar	15
Herbs and their Beneficial Properties	5
Homemade Chicken Stock	63
Italian Dressing	86
Pumpkin Soup - A "Harvest Hug"	53
Red, White and Blue Burgers	40
Shepard's Pie with an Herbal Flare	38

S

Sage

Chicken Root Stew	80
Classic Basil Pesto	28
Compound Butter	61
Drop Herb Biscuits	75
Fresh Corn Chowder	36
Herbal Infused Vinegar	15
Herbs and their beneficial properties	5
Homemade Chicken Stock	63
Lydia's Potato Soup w/Dumplings	23
Pumpkin Soup - A "Harvest Hug"	53

Sausage

Dinner in a Pumpkin	58
Dutch Harvest Chili	55
Mother's Meatballs	30
Stuffed Dates	84
Vegetable Lasagna	34

Spinach

Chicken Root Stew	80
Classic Apple Salad w/an Herbal Twist	52

Classic Basil Pesto	28
Fresh Spinach & Spring Asparagus Quiche	19
Fresh Spinach Salad with "a Lil Oink"	22
Steak Florentine	78

Star Anise
Difference between infusion & decoction	8
Hot Mulled Wassail	74

Strawberries
Avocado - Blueberry & Basil Ice Cream	12
Good Morning Smoothie	42
Herbal Infused Vinegar	15
Rustic Strawberry Tart	41

Squash
Garden Pasta Salad	45
Three Sisters	87
Vegetable Lasagna	34

T

Thyme
Apple Thyme Salad Dressing	85
Chicken Root Stew	80
Christmas Honey-Thyme Cookies	76
Classic Apple Salad w/an Herbal Twist	52
Compound Butter	61
Creamy Ranch Dressing	85
Edible Flowers	16
Herbal Fun Facts	13
Herbal Infused Vinegar	15
Herbs and their Beneficial Properties	5
Homemade Chicken Stock	63
Italian Dressing	86
Pumpkin Soup - A "Harvest Hug"	53

Shepard's Pie with an Herbal Flare	38

Tomatoes
Around the World Tomatoes	31
Classic Caprese Salad	32
Dutch Harvest Chili	55
Garden Pasta Salad	45
Homemade Ketchup	39
Mango Salsa	29
Mickey's Spaghetti Sauce	30
Ratatouille	43
Red, White and Blue Burgers	40
Steak Florentine	78
Zucchini Frittata with Mint & Basil	20

Tomatoes
Asparagus Roll-Ups	44
Stuffed Dates	84
Stuffed Pepper (Mango) Soup	33
Turkey/Game Day Cranberry Relish	66

V

Vanilla
Baked Pears with Cranberry Sauce	72
Celebration Rum Cake	69
Christmas Honey-Thyme Cookies	76
French Toast Bake	59
Good Morning Smoothie	42
Homemade Hot Cocoa	75

Z

Zucchini
Ratatouille	43
Zucchini Frittata with Mint & Basil	20

*Of course with any new herb, herbal remedy, herbal supplement or herbal recipe, one should always consult their healthcare professional before trying, taking or using any new herb. I cannot stress the importance of proper herbal identification enough. When growing, harvesting or foraging for herbs if you are not 100% positive as to what you are using, just don't. Always remember, "when in doubt, leave it out!" *Julia Brown and/or A Simpler Thyme Ltd. is not a healthcare provider or facility.*

www.ingramcontent.com/pod-product-compliance
Lightning Source LLC
Chambersburg PA
CBHW042056050526
44107CB00110B/1191